Andrew James Campbell Allen

The Protestation Issued by the English Romanists in 1788

Andrew James Campbell Allen

The Protestation Issued by the English Romanists in 1788

ISBN/EAN: 9783744773362

Printed in Europe, USA, Canada, Australia, Japan

Cover: Foto ©Thomas Meinert / pixelio.de

More available books at **www.hansebooks.com**

THE PROTESTATION

ISSUED BY THE ENGLISH ROMANISTS

IN 1788.

EDITED, WITH INTRODUCTION AND NOTES,

BY THE

REV. A. J. C. ALLEN, M.A.

VICAR OF S. MARY'S-THE-LESS, CAMBRIDGE,
FORMERLY FELLOW AND ASSISTANT TUTOR OF PETERHOUSE.

———————

PUBLISHED UNDER THE DIRECTION OF THE TRACT COMMITTEE.

———————

LONDON :

SOCIETY FOR PROMOTING CHRISTIAN KNOWLEDGE,

NORTHUMBERLAND AVENUE, W.C.; 43, QUEEN VICTORIA STREET, E.C.

BRIGHTON: 129, NORTH STREET.

NEW YORK: E. & J. B. YOUNG & CO.

1897.

PREFACE.

— •• —

My object in publishing this edition of the
Protestation of 1788 is a very simple and very
humble one. In the first place I hope it will
recall to the minds of some what is certainly
a very interesting episode in the history of
religious thought in this country, and in the
second place I trust it will help Englishmen to
understand that the contrast which Roman
controversialists are so fond of drawing between
the unity of thought and belief that are said to
prevail amongst Romanists on the one side, and
the dissensions which rend the English Church
on the other, has no genuine basis of fact to rest
on. There can be no doubt that the picture of
unity and agreement on the Roman side has
been one of the chief causes that have unsettled
the faith of a certain number of Anglicans in

A 2

these latter days, and attracted them to desert their true mother in the belief that in the communion of Rome they would find rest from religious disputes and the bitterness of party strife. Of course those who have known anything of the inner life of Romanism have known that this picture of unity is purely a creation of the imagination, that party strife has been quite as rife in Roman as in Anglican circles, and the recently published *Life of the late Cardinal Manning* has shown that Roman feuds are embittered by personal considerations in a way that is quite strange to Anglicans. But though this is well known to those who read large books like *The Life of Manning*, there is a numerous class of persons deeply interested in religious questions whose knowledge, and whose power of acquiring knowledge, as to the true bearing of debated questions and the real inner life of different communions is comparatively limited, and on them an astute Romanist may still produce a deep impression by exhibiting the beauties of his imaginary picture. I trust that the present publication may help to open the eyes of some, and make them feel that it is better to abide where God has placed them rather than seek relief from their troubles in an imaginary paradise, where in truth instead of a continual unbroken peace they will find a state of perpetual strife and warfare, and that on questions which are certainly not unimportant.

A. J. C. A.

CAMBRIDGE,

December 11, 1896.

CONTENTS.

INTRODUCTION.

In the year 1570 Pius V issued the famous Bull *Regnans in Excelsis*. In this he calls Elizabeth "the pretended Queen of England," and goes on to recount how she "usurping the place of supreme head [1] of the Church in all England, and his [i. e. the Pope's] chief authority and jurisdiction, recalled her kingdom, lately brought back to the catholic faith, and the good fruits thereof, to miserable loss. . . . And having dared to decide concerning affairs of the Church, forbade the prelates, clergy, and people to recognize the Roman Church, and compelled many to abjure the authority and obedience of

---

[1] It is worth notice as illustrating the Pope's historical accuracy, that when Elizabeth came to the throne, she repudiated the title of Supreme Head of the Church as being too high for any human being, and substituted for it that of Supreme Governor. Henry VIII, Edward VI, and Mary, who is praised in the Bull for having brought back the realm of England to obedience to the Roman See, all accepted the title without question.

the Roman Pontiff and to recognize her as mistress in matters both temporal and spiritual. . . . Therefore supported by His authority, who willed to place us, although unequal to so great a work, in this supreme throne of justice, we declare with the fullness of apostolic power that the aforesaid Elizabeth is a heretic and favourer of heretics, and that they who adhere to her are condemned with the same anathemas, and are cut off from the unity of the body of Christ; that she herself too is deprived of her pretended right to the aforesaid kingdom; and that the nobles, and commons of the said kingdom and all others who have in any way taken an oath to her are for ever absolved from any such oath, and all manner of duty, allegiance and obedience, and by the authority of these presents we do also absolve them; and we deprive the said Elizabeth of her pretended right to the kingdom and to all other things aforesaid. And we command and charge all and singular, the nobles, commons, peoples, and others aforesaid not to dare to obey her or her orders, mandates and laws. And those who will act otherwise we include in the same sentence of anathema [1]."

[1] The Bull is printed at length in Cardwell's *Documentary Annals*, i. pp. 328–331, and the chief parts are given by Prothero in his *Statutes and Constitutional Documents*, 1559–1625, p. 195. In 1580, Gregory XIII, the successor of Pius, issued

Now this Bull clearly contains the following assumptions :—

1. The Pope claims for himself " jurisdiction " over the Church of England.

an explanation of the Bull, which enacted "that the same should always bind the queen and the heretics : but that the Catholics it should by no means bind, as matters then stood or were : but thereafter, when the public execution of that Bull might be had or made." On the eve of the sailing of the Armada, Sixtus V issued a Bull in which he "renewed the sentence of Pius V, and Gregory XIII, touching and concerning the deposition of Elizabeth, whom he excommunicated and deposed anew from all royal dignity, and from the title, right and pretension to the crown, of the kingdom of England and Ireland, declaring her illegitimate, and an usurper of the said kingdoms, discharging the subjects of the said kingdom and all others from all obedience, from the oath of fidelity, and from all in which they could be obliged to her, or to any one in her name."

The comments of Charles Butler—from whose *Memoirs* the quotations in this note are taken—on these Bulls seems to be worth quoting. Speaking of the Bull of Pius, he says : "Such was this celebrated Bull, ever to be condemned and ever to be lamented. It is most clear that the Pope assumed by it a right, the exercise of which Christ had explicitly disclaimed for Himself : that it tended to produce a civil war between the queen's Protestant and Catholic subjects, and all the horrors of a disputed succession, and that it could not but involve a multitude of respectable and conscientious individuals in the bitterest and most complicated distress. What could have fascinated the pontiff, virtuous and pious, as all historians describe him, to the adoption of such a measure?"
Again : "The mention of these Bulls must be painful to a Catholic, but it is an historical obligation, and when he mentions them it is a duty to condemn them. It is pleasing to add, that they were disregarded by the generality of the

2. This jurisdiction extends to the power to
declare that the reigning sovereign has no right
to her position, and not only to absolve all her
subjects from their oaths of allegiance but even
to forbid them under pain of anathema obeying
her laws.

These claims on the part of the Papacy were
nothing new in 1570. In February, 1076,
Gregory VII [Hildebrand] held a consistory in
the Lateran Palace, and issued a Bull condemn-
ing the Emperor Henry IV. Gregory began his
Bull with a long address to S. Peter, and then
went on. "In full confidence in the authority
over all Christian people, granted by God to the
delegate of S. Peter, for the honour and defence
of the Church, in the name of Almighty God, the
Father, the Son and the Holy Ghost, and by the
power and authority of S. Peter, I interdict King
Henry, son of Henry[1] the Emperor, who in his
unexampled pride has risen against the Church,

Catholics of England " (*Historical Memoirs*, vol. i. pp. 188, 190).
The difficulty of the English Romanists truly was great.
Papal Bulls (see Note 5) have the force of Canon Law, and
Canon Law is binding in conscience, in other words the
Canon Law claims to be the voice of God, while the law of
the State is only the voice of man. The large majority of
the English Romanists of the time chose to follow the voice
of man and the Romanists of two centuries later praise them
for it !

[1] Henry III who died in 1056, and was succeeded by his
son Henry IV.

from the government of the whole realm of
Germany and of Italy. I absolve all Christians
from the oaths which they have sworn or may
swear to him : and I forbid all obedience to him
as king. For it is just that he who impugns the
honour of the Church should himself forfeit all
the honour that he seems to have : and because
he has scorned the obedience of a Christian and
not returned to the Lord from whom he had
revolted by holding communion with the excommunicate, by committing many iniquities, and
despising the admonitions which as thou [i. e.
S. Peter] knowest I have given him for his
salvation, and has separated himself from the
Church by creating schism : I bind him therefore in thy name in the bonds of anathema ;
that all nations may know and may acknowledge that thou art Peter, that upon thy rock
the Son of the living God has built His Church,
and that the gates of hell shall not prevail
against it [1]."

In 1212 Innocent III issued an interdict
deposing King John of England, handing the
kingdom over to Lewis of France, and calling on
all John's subjects to rise in arms to aid the
French king. Three years later the deposing
power was formally asserted in the Canons of
the Fourth Lateran Council.

[1] Quoted in Milman, *Latin Christianity*, iv. pp. 78, 79.

In 1302 Boniface VIII held a Consistory at Rome and spoke as follows with reference to Philip the Fair, King of France :—" But for us the King would not have a foot in the stirrup. When the English, the Germans, all his more powerful vassals, rose up against him in one league, to whom but to us did he owe his triumph ? Our predecessors have deposed three kings of France. These things are written in their annals as in ours : and this king guilty of so much more heinous offences, we could depose as we could discharge a groom, though we should do it with sorrow. As for the citation of Bishops, we could call the whole world to our presence, weak and aged as we are. If they come not at our command let them know that they are hereby deprived and deposed." In the famous Bull *Unam Sanctam* which was issued from this same Consistory the Pope speaks in the same sense. "There are two swords, the spiritual and the temporal : our Lord said not of these two swords ' It is too much ' but ' It is enough.' Both are in the power of the Church : the one, the spiritual, to be used by the Church, the other, the material, to be used for the Church : the former that of priests, the latter that of kings and soldiers, to be wielded at the command and by the sufferance of the priest. One sword must be under the other, the temporal

under the spiritual. . . . The spiritual instituted
the temporal power and judges whether that
power is well exercised. . . . If the temporal
power errs it is judged by the spiritual. To
deny this is to assert, with the heretical Mani-
chaeans, two co-equal principles. We therefore
assert, define, and pronounce, that it is necessary
to salvation to believe that every human being
is subject to the Roman Pontiff[1]."

It was acting in the spirit of these last words
that Innocent IV in 1250 had handed over the
kingdom of the Two Sicilies to Edmund, son of
Henry III of England. Innocent's claim indeed
did not go quite so far as that of Boniface, inasmuch as the Sicilies were Christian kingdoms,
but in 1493 Alexander VI took the teaching of
Boniface in its extreme literalness, and issued
a Bull dividing the whole of the recently dis-
covered world of America between the kings of
Spain and Portugal. The practical results of this
award were felt for long. As late as 1789 the
claims of Spain, which were founded on it, nearly
led to war between that country and England,
owing to some English traders having settled on
Vancouver's Island, which the Spaniards claimed
as being in that part of the New World which
the Pope had given to them.

[1] The speech and Bull are quoted in Milman, vii. pp. 124,
125.

In attempting to depose Elizabeth then and to absolve her subjects from their oaths of allegiance, Pius V and his successors were acting on principles which had long been held and often acted on by the Supreme Pontiffs. It is indeed the last occasion on which any attempt to use the deposing power has been made. But though the exercise of the power has been practically abandoned, the right to it continued long, if it does not even continue still, to be claimed at Rome. Thus Ferraris in the article Papa in the ninth edition [1] of his *Prompta Bibliotheca*, a large and authoritative Theological Dictionary, writes:—" Whence princes and kings, who are infidels, can by the sentence of the Pope in certain cases be deprived of the dominion which they have over the faithful, as, if they have occupied by force the lands of Christians, or strive to turn those of their subjects who are faithful from the faith and such like, as is clearly shown by Cardinal Bellarmine in his *Apologia contra Regem Angliae*, cap. iv."

Suarez [2] is perhaps even more emphatic : "For thus," he writes in his *Defensio Fidei Catho-*

---

[1] This edition was published in 1782.

[2] Francisco Suarez (1548–1617) was a distinguished Jesuit and teacher of theology at several Universities, including Rome. The treatise from which the extracts in the text are taken was written in 1613 at the command of the Pope.

licae et Apostolicae adversus Anglicanae Sectae Errores, lib. vi. cap. v. sec. 2, " the subjects of any heretic, on the ground that he is publicly denounced as a heretic by a legitimate sentence, are freed from their oath of fealty by the decree of Gregory IX in cap. ult. *De Haereticis;* and S. Thomas, 2, 2, q. 12, art. 2, explains the power of inflicting that punishment and the most just reason of it. Similarly that any one is absolved from the bond of an oath of fealty given to a lord, who is publicly excommunicated and denounced, is shown by Urban II, in cap. ult. 15, q. 6 ; and Gregory VII, with the Roman synod, says the same thing in cap. *Nos Sanctorum.* And here the bond of the oath is not simply and completely taken away, but, as it were, suspended for the time during which the excommunicate continues contumacious. But this is not the case when the king or ruler is deposed and deprived of the rule over his kingdom on account of heresy or other crimes, for then it is entirely taken away, and, as it were, its material is taken away and it is rendered void. And in this way Innocent IV, with the Council of Lyons, absolved all the vassals of the Emperor Frederick from their oath of fealty; and other examples have been given above, by which the ancient and universal sense of the Church, which is the best interpreter of Scripture, is shown."

And again:—"Although the Pontiff cannot punish a heathen[1] king, he can free those of his subjects who are faithful from his dominion. This title seemed to S. Thomas and approved theologians so weighty and efficacious, that by itself it would suffice to deprive an infidel king of his dominion and power over the faithful, even if the former reason of vindictive and just punishment should cease to hold. For, according to the doctrine of Paul, the Church does not judge concerning those who are without. Whence the some theologians infer that the Pontiff cannot punish a heathen[1] king who is not baptized on account of his infidelity or other sins. But, nevertheless, if he has faithful subjects he can snatch them from subjection to him on account of the moral and clear danger of perversion, as S. Thomas teaches, 2, 2, q. 10, art. 10, and infers from Paul, 1 Cor. vi.[2]"

In our own day Messrs. Addis and Arnold, in their *Catholic Dictionary*, have written in much the same strain. They say:—"After her [i. e. Elizabeth's] death, nothing similar occurs, and yet the conditions of Catholics in England grew worse from reign to reign, and it is notorious

---

[1] *Ethnicus.* There is no English word which will exactly give the meaning. It includes not only the "heathen," but Christians who are outside the pale of the Roman Communion.

[2] *Works*, ed. 1859, vol. xxiv. pp. 683, 321.

that the doctrine, on which the Bull rests, continued to be held in Rome." As the same writers aver, the dropping of the use of this power is not due to any change in will, or to the Pope's learning that the claim is one to which he has no right, but to the great political changes that have come over Europe in the last three centuries.

The Bull of 1570 is interesting, then, as marking the last occasion on which the popes have tried to put into practice the rights which, at least since the days of Hildebrand, they have claimed as their own, but it is specially interesting to Englishmen because its issue marks an epoch in the history of their branch of the Catholic Church. When it appeared Elizabeth had been twelve years on the throne. During the greater part of that time there had been no open schism in England. There were then, as always, parties in the Church. There was the great bulk of the nation who were fairly content with the state of things that had been brought about by Elizabeth and Parker; there was the party, consisting largely of those who had been driven into exile in the evil days of Mary, who had drunk in largely the principles of the continental reformers, and had returned to their native land anxious to carry forward the English Reformation on lines similar to those introduced by Calvin at Geneva; lastly, there was the party

who felt that things had gone too far, who were
anxious to bring the Church back to the condition
she had been in, in the latter days of Henry VIII,
and who had come to think that the only safety
against further change and the return of days
like those of Edward VI, lay in the acknowledge-
ment of the authority of the Pope. These parties
were all inside the Church. They frequented
their parish churches and accepted the ministra-
tion of the clergy of the Church. The first open
schism came in 1568. In that year a congregation of separatists was formed in London, on
congregational principles, under the leadership
of a clergyman by name Robert Brown. Two
years later the Bull appeared. The position
hitherto held by those who clung to the old
state of things was no longer tenable. They
were forced to make their choice. They must
either definitely throw in their lot with the bulk
of their countrymen and become loyal Church-
men, or they must throw in their lot with the
Pope, separate themselves from their parish
churches, and enjoy such worship as they might
be able to provide for themselves. Such is the
origin of the Roman schism in this country.
Those who obeyed the Pope with any logical
consistency became not only schismatics, but
traitors as well. Happily men are not ruled by
logic, and many of those who separated from the

Church remained loyal to their queen and country. The most prominent of these was Lord Howard of Effingham, who led the English fleet to victory over the Armada, and delivered England for ever from the fear of being reduced to the subjection of the Roman yoke. It would have been wise, no doubt, for the Government of the day to have recognized in its fullness the distinction between the loyal and disloyal Romanists, to have treated the former with all leniency and the latter with the severity they deserved. But men in the face of great dangers are scarcely likely to recognize distinctions like these, and if, in the latter days of Elizabeth, all Romanists were put under the ban of persecution, it is clear that the Government of the queen acted under the greatest provocation. In 1568 the English Seminary was founded at Douai by William Allen, who had been a Fellow of Oriel College, Oxford, and afterwards became a cardinal. The object of the college was to train priests to come over to England and pro-pagate Romanism. The first missionaries were two Jesuit Fathers—Parsons and Campion—who landed in 1580, and were quickly followed by a host of others. These men were no doubt largely influenced by religious zeal and the desire to bring back to the faith those who they believed had fallen into heresy. They carried their lives in their hands and endured suffering with great courage. But there was a large political element in their work too. There is no doubt that many of them were centres of sedition, and on the eve of the coming of the Armada, Parsons and Allen issued a book openly advocating the cause of the King of Spain. Such conduct, at a time when the country seemed to be in extreme peril, and to have little hope of escape from the enemies that were arming against her, goes far to explain how that hatred of Rome and everything Roman, which had been burnt into the English character in the days of Mary, became so fixed and permanent.

At the accession of James I, the hopes of the Romanists and of the other dissenters rose high. Under the new king they looked for liberty and consideration, but they found none. The hopes of the Romanists were shattered by Gunpowder treason, the laws against them were made severer than before, and the persecution to a large extent changed its character. The political element grew weaker and the religious one more prominent. After 1745 the former disappeared entirely. The Romanists were then a very small body in the country; they had come loyally to accept the Hanoverian dynasty, and had given up all idea of raising sedition against the Government. Under these circumstances the retention of the penal laws which prevented Romanists taking part in the civil life of the country, and forbad them the enjoyment of the rites of their religion, was quite unjustifiable.

It is true that, with characteristic English inconsistency, the evil was, in practice, a good deal mitigated. So long as they kept in the background and abstained from proselytizing, the Romanists were allowed to carry on their worship unmolested, and the episcopal vicars-apostolic, who were sent to govern them, lived freely in the country. Still they had much cause for complaint, and with the growing spirit of toleration it was only a question of time how soon they would obtain the complete freedom which they at present enjoy. As early as 1757 a certain measure of relief was given to the Romanists in Ireland, and in 1771 a Bill was passed which repealed part of a very oppressive Act which had been enacted after the Revolution. This Act was the starting-point for further relief. In 1782 a meeting of the principal Romanists in England appointed a committee of five "to promote and attend to the affairs of the Catholic body in England," and five years later the committee was enlarged to ten. Mr. Charles Butler was secretary to both committees. In his *Historical Memoirs* respecting the English, Irish, and Scottish Romanists he has left us a full account of the proceedings of the committee, and it is from the second volume of his work that the Protestation here reprinted is taken.

The committee of ten held a meeting on May 9, 1788. Lord Petre, Sir Henry Charles Englefield, and Mr. Fermor reported that they had, that morning, had an interview with the Prime Minister, Mr. Pitt ; that he had expressed himself favourably with reference to their claims for relief, but wished the committee to furnish him with answers to the following questions for the information of the Government :—

" 1. Has the Pope, or cardinals, or any body of men, or any individual of the Church of Rome, any civil authority, power, jurisdiction, or pre-eminence whatsoever within the realm of England ?

" 2. Can the Pope, or cardinals, or any body of men, or any individual of the Church of Rome, absolve or dispense with his majesty's subjects from their oath of allegiance upon any pretext whatsoever ?

" 3. Is there any principle in the tenets of the Catholic faith by which Catholics are justified in not keeping faith with heretics, or other persons differing from them in religious opinions, in any transaction either of a public or private nature[1] ?"

The facts of history referred to, and the papal

[1] Butler's *Memoirs*, ii. p. 110.

Bulls already quoted in this Introduction, supply a very clear and definite answer to the first two of these questions. The third is a matter of moral theology, and to answer it, it is necessary to quote the teaching of some acknowledged authorities of the Roman Church on the point. Thus Ferraris in his article *Haereticus* [1] writes, " Heretics lose jurisdiction and authority over their vassals and servants ; for the vassals and servants and others are freed from private obligations due to heretics and from keeping faith with them, as is taught in a clear text in cap. *Absolutos* 16 *De Haereticis.*"

The " clear text " referred to by Ferraris is to be found in the fifth book, Tit. vii, of the *Collection of Canon Law*, drawn up by Pope Gregory IX [A.D. 1227–1241], and runs as follows:—

" Let those who are held bound by any compact, established with any surety, with those who have openly fallen into heresy, know that they are absolved from the debt of human faith and all obedience."

Other authorities might easily be quoted, and, on the whole, it does not appear that the committee need have found any difficulty in answering the points on which the Prime Minister wished for information. But the answers, which they would have obtained, by an appeal

[1] Tom. iii. p. 557.

to history, and to the teaching of accredited doctors, on the obligations due to heretics, would not at all have helped forward the cause which the committee had at heart. It was necessary for their purpose that they should be able to answer the three questions in the negative. Accordingly, they adopted a method of obtaining answers which had first been employed by Henry VIII in connexion with his divorce proceedings. The three questions were sent to the Universities of Sorbonne, Louvain, Douai, Alcola, and Salamanca, and a unanimous answer in the following terms was returned by them:—

" 1. That the Pope, or cardinals, or any body of men, or any individual of the Church of Rome. has not, nor have, any civil authority, power, or jurisdiction, or pre-eminence whatsoever within the realm of England.

" 2. That the Pope, or cardinals, or any body of men, or any individual of the Church of Rome, cannot absolve or dispense with his majesty's subjects from their oath of allegiance upon any pretext whatsoever.

" 3. That there is no principle in the tenets of the Catholic faith by which Catholics are justified in not keeping faith with heretics, or other persons differing from them in religious opinions, in any transactions either of a public or private nature."

These answers were duly submitted to Mr. Pitt. But it was felt that it was important to try to set the English people, as well as the Government, right on these points. A strong prejudice against granting any relief to the Romanists existed, because Englishmen commonly attributed to them the opinions that had been constantly proclaimed by popes and councils and doctors, and it was essential to get rid of this prejudice if much progress was really to be made. The Protestation which is here reprinted was accordingly drawn up in the end of 1788. It was signed by all the four vicars-apostolic who then ruled in the Church in the four districts into which England had been divided. " With a very inconsiderable exception, the Protestation was signed by all the Catholic clergy and laity in England of any note. In the public prints it was circulated throughout the country. It was received with general approbation. In 1789 it was signed in London at a general meeting of the English Catholics by every person present [1]."

The Protestation speaks for itself. The English Romanists were resolved that no one should mistake what they meant. They embodied the opinions given by the foreign universities in very strong and unmistakeable language, and in some directions they added to them. They

[1] Butler's *Historical Memoirs*, ii. p. 122.

repudiate the idea "that the Pope, by virtue of his spiritual power, can dispense with the obligations of any compact or oath taken or entered into by a Catholic;" and "that not only the Pope, but even a Catholic priest has power to pardon the sins of Catholics at his will and pleasure." What it seems necessary to say on these points will be found in the notes. But there is one statement which, from the importance that it has acquired in recent years, calls for some further comment. The signatories to the Protestation plainly state, " We acknowledge no infallibility in the Pope." As is well known, the infallibility of the Pope was defined as an article of faith at the Vatican Council in 1870. Since that time any one who ventures to question the dogma is liable to excommunication. After the council Döllinger, the most learned theologian of the Roman communion, and several other pious and learned men actually were excommunicated because they refused to accept the dogma. All that is well known, but what perhaps is not so well known is that the council claimed that they were in no sense adding a new dogma to the faith, but were only defining what had been handed down by constant tradition as part of the faith [1].

[1] Cf. the statement of Leo XIII in the recently issued Encyclical *Satis Cognitum*, § 15:—" In the decree of the

It is clear that if this teaching is right, if the
council only defined what had always been part
of the faith of the Church, the English Romanists,
both priests and people, in the end of the last
century had fallen away into error and heresy.
But if so, they sinned in good company. They
were not the first, and they were not the last of
those whom Rome has looked on as her faithful
children, and who have yet doubted or denied
the infallibility of her bishop.

J. Benigne Bossuet, Bishop of Meaux [1681–
1704], was the most distinguished divine that
the Church of France has perhaps ever produced.
In 1682 a general assembly of the bishops and
clergy of France was held to consider the
relations between the Church and State. The
assembly resolved that a declaration should be
drawn up stating the views held by the Church
of France on the questions at issue, and particularly on the limits of the authority of the
Pope. The preparation of the declaration was
entrusted to the Bishops of Tournay and Meaux.
The two, however, soon found that they could
not agree. The difference arose with regard to
the question of infallibility. The Bishop of
Tournay maintained that not only could indivi-

Vatican Council as to the nature and authority of the primacy
of the Roman Pontiff, no newly conceived opinion is set
forth, but the venerable and constant belief of every age."

dual popes fall into error, but that the Roman
see might itself become apostate, as some celebrated Eastern sees had actually done. Bossuet
accepted the first of these statements, but he
would not admit the second. He held, that the
protecting hand of God would lead the Roman
see quickly to recognize any errors into which
her bishops might fall, and to repudiate their
teaching. In the end the Bishop of Tournay
withdrew from the work, and the celebrated
Declaration of the Gallican Clergy was drawn up
by Bossuet alone. This declaration contains the
four famous propositions known as the Gallican
Liberties. The fourth of these has reference to the
question of infallibility, and runs as follows :—

"The Pope has the principal place in deciding
questions of faith, and his decrees extend to
every church and all churches ; but nevertheless
his judgement is not irreversible until confirmed
by the consent of the Church."

The declaration, after its adoption by the
Assembly of Clergy, naturally gave rise to much
controversy. Bossuet prepared an elaborate
defence of it, which, however, was not published .
till some years after his death. We are not
concerned here with the questions that were in
dispute between the Pope and Louis XIV. The
special point of interest is to see how far the
Vatican dogma was accepted in the Church of

France in the end of the seventeenth century. The proposition quoted above and two brief extracts from Bossuet will make this clear.

" Here we wish to make clear the true meaning of the Gallican Declaration. The Gallican Fathers did not put it forward that the Roman pontiff should not be held to be infallible, a matter about which there are such great disputings in the schools. They put far away these scholastic voices and questionings. They did not think they belonged to the episcopal order. They preferred to look to matters of practice, and to put down as certain, however the scholastic and subtle question might be settled, what was agreed upon among all Catholics, that a decree of the pontiffs is not to be held irreformable, nor to have gained its complete strength, unless it has received the consent of the Church. And when this opinion is established, the whole question of infallibility is put amongst matters that are speculative and vain."

Again : " And so, at any rate, the doctrine which denies the superiority and infallibility of the pontiff is free from all blame, which is sufficient for the question before us [1]."

To enforce his view Bossuet discusses at length several cases in which popes before his time had fallen into error.

[1] *Works* of Bossuet, ed. 1818, vol. xxxiii. pp. 396, 635.

In the middle of the last century the Irish Romanists, in their agitation for toleration, put forward views very similar to those contained in the English Protestation, and indeed it is only since 1870 that a belief in papal infallibility seems to have commonly prevailed in these islands. In the years preceding the granting of Catholic emancipation, the Irish Roman Catholic bishops were examined before a Parliamentary Committee as to the views they held regarding the temporal authority of the Pope. Archbishop Murray, in reply to a question whether the Irish bishops adopted or rejected the Gallican Liberties, "said, · These liberties have not come under their consideration as a body. The Irish Catholic bishops have, therefore, not either adopted or rejected them. They have adopted, however, and that on their oaths, the leading doctrines which these liberties contain; that is, the doctrines which reject the deposing power of the popes and their right to interfere with the temporalities of princes. That is distinctly recognized not as one of the Gallican Liberties, but as a doctrine which the Gospel teaches.' Bishop Doyle said that if the Pope were to intermeddle with the temporal rights of the king, they would oppose him even by the exercise of their spiritual authority; that is, as he explained it, by preaching the Gospel to the people, and instructing them, in such a case, to oppose the Pope. Besides this repudiation of the temporal power of the Pope, these bishops declared their opinion that the authority of the Pope in spiritual matters was limited by the canons and by the councils, and they swore, as they could then with truth, that the doctrine of the Pope's personal infallibility was no part of the Christian faith [1]."

A book which has been much relied upon in Ireland as a controversial authority, and which was published with the approval of both the Scottish and Irish Roman bishops, is Keenan's *Catechism*. The copies that were issued before 1870 contained the following question and answer:—

" *Q.* Must not Catholics believe the Pope in himself to be infallible ?

A. This is a Protestant invention ; it is no article of the Catholic faith ; no decision of his can oblige, under pain of heresy, unless it be received and enforced by the teaching body; that is, by the bishops of the Church."

Keenan's *Catechism* is still in circulation, but the copies which have been issued since 1870 do not contain the above question and answer.

That this is the true state of the case, that before 1870 papal infallibility was a matter of

---

[1] Salmon, *Infallibility of the Church*, p. 264.

opinion and not of faith, that the dogma was
held by some and denied by others who were
regarded equally as the loyal sons of Rome, is
indeed well known and can hardly be better
stated than in the following extract from the
late Cardinal Wiseman's Essay on *The High
Church Theory of Dogmatical Authority* :—

" The Catholic Church holds a dogma often
proclaimed, that in defining matters of faith she
is infallible. No one would be allowed by her
to teach any other doctrine ; whoever does
ceases practically to be a Catholic ; and if he
be a pastor, and prove obstinate in his error,
must be removed from his office. At the same
time, while all agree that this infallibility resides
in the unanimous suffrage of the Church, whether
united in council or dispersed over the world,
the Italian doctrine extends it to the plenitude
of authority residing in its head, and makes his
dogmatical decrees of force antecedently to the
expressed consent, or implied acquiescence, of
the other pastors. The Gallican denies this, and
maintains that time must be given for the Church
to assent or dissent; and only in the case of
assent considers the decree binding. Practically,
as experience has proved, either opinion leads to
the same results ; but manifestly the assertors
of neither can demand that their peculiar theory
be received by others, as the defined or ac-

knowledged principle of the Church, neither
think we that they could reasonably charge with
' misunderstanding their Church's doctrines' such
as would not receive it [1]."

The history of the sequel to the issue of the
Protestation may be soon told. In the course of
1789 a Bill was drawn up which Mr. Mitford
agreed to introduce into Parliament in the next
session. The heads of the Bill were published
in the papers, but there were two points in it
which aroused a good deal of opposition from
some of the English Romanists, particularly the
vicars-apostolic.

1. The Bill contained an oath which was to
be taken by all Romanists. The oath was
founded on the Protestation and indeed was
a repetition of a good deal of it, but in one
clause there was a modification. The Protestation contained the statement, "That no
church nor any prelate, nor any assembly of
prelates or priests, nor any ecclesiastical power
whatsoever, have, hath, or ought to have, any
jurisdiction or authority whatsoever within this
realm that can directly or indirectly affect or
interfere with the independence, sovereignty,
laws, constitution or government thereof; or
the rights, liberties, persons, or properties of the
people of the said realm or any of them." The

[1] *Essays* by his Eminence Cardinal Wiseman, vol. ii. p. 122.

corresponding part of the oath ran as follows :—
" That no foreign prince, person, prelate, state, or
potentate, hath or ought to have any civil jurisdiction or authority whatsoever within this realm;
or any spiritual authority, power, or jurisdiction
whatsoever that can directly or indirectly interfere with the independence, sovereignty, laws, or
constitution of this kingdom, or with the civil
or ecclesiastical government thereof, as by law
established, or with the rights, liberties, persons,
or properties of the subjects thereof."

2. The Bill described the English Romanists
as " protesting Catholic dissenters."

The plain reader will wonder on what grounds,
those who had signed the Protestation, could
object to these things. The Protestation re-
pudiates any authority in the Pope or others
that can interfere with the civil government of
the nation or the rights of individuals. The
oath specifies this authority as either civil or
spiritual. The change does not seem to be
material. In the last resort the Pope's claims
rest on his spiritual authority as the vicar of
Christ, and if the Popes have claimed to depose
princes and give away kingdoms they have used
spiritual weapons [1], and professed to have in view

---

[1] Of course the Popes have perpetually, when they had the
opportunity, used material aids in the shape of princes and
armies to gain their ends, but the secular arm has always

spiritual ends. Hence if the Romanist repudiated the civil authority of the Popes while maintaining a spiritual authority that could interfere in civil matters, it does not appear that their protestations of loyalty would be worth much. Charles Butler and the Catholic committee were acting in all good faith, and therefore agreed to the proposed form of oath to make it clear that they had no reservations in mind, that were not on the surface. But the vicars-apostolic had other ideas. On Oct. 21, 1789, they signed an encyclical letter, addressed by them to all the clergy and laity in their districts, in which they declared that "after mature deliberation and previous discussion, they unanimously condemned the new form of an oath intended for the Catholics ... and declared it unlawful to be taken [1]." They also expressed their total disapproval of the appellation given to the Roman Catholics in the Bill.

The committee then agreed to alter the oath to agree exactly with the Protestation, but even that was not approved, and after a good deal of discussion and some recrimination the Bill was finally passed in 1791. The oath which it contained repudiated only the temporal or civil

been invoked to enforce the spiritual decrees. The spiritual authority is at the base of everything.

[1] Butler's *Memoirs*, vol. ii. p. 123.

jurisdiction of the Pope, and says nothing of spiritual jurisdiction or of anything that may flow from it. A loophole was thus left open. How far that loophole may be extended may be learnt from some of the doings of modern Romanists.

The State in England has always claimed, and I suppose most Englishmen will believe rightly claimed, the power to regulate the conditions on which property shall be held, and in particular the conditions on which property left or given for charitable or religious purposes shall be retained and used. It was in the exercise of this power that the celebrated Mortmain Acts were passed in the time of Edward I and his successors. The Statutes of Mortmain were followed by those of Provisors and Praemunire, which, though not dealing with property so directly, had yet much to do with it, as they were intended to prevent the Popes appropriating the English benefices for the support of foreign ecclesiastics. These Acts were a source of more or less continuous friction between the Popes and the English Church. Martin V tried to override them altogether, and " provided " candidates for a number of English sees and other benefices. When his unlawful doings were resisted, he wrote an angry letter to the archbishops of Canterbury and York, calling upon them to disregard the offensive statutes, " which," said he, " inasmuch as they are expressly against the liberty of the Church, we declare to have been and to be condemned and reprobated."

This is ancient history. It is referred to here on account of the curious analogy which is afforded to it by the doings of the Romanists in our own day. In 1860 the Charity Commission was called into being, and all property held on trust for charitable or religious purposes was required to be enrolled with the commissioners, and the accounts of the receipts and expenditure to be regularly furnished to them. The object of Parliament was to prevent abuses, and to secure that all trust property shall be duly looked after and applied to the purposes for which it was intended. The question was at once raised as to whether the Romanists should obey the law or set it aside. Some of the bishops who inherited the tradition of those who drew up the Protestation, and who would not allow their obedience to the Pope to interfere with their allegiance to the State, were in favour of yielding, but Cardinal Wiseman and the Ultramontane party took another line. To register their trusts might be a dangerous experiment. Many of them were held in spite of the Statutes of Mortmain, and would therefore, if they were disclosed, be liable to confiscation. The matter was referred to Rome for settlement, and in 1862 the Roman Court gave its decision. That decision was in favour of the views of the Ultramontanes. It was held " that in all cases where the trust property would be placed in jeopardy by registration, the charitable trusts were not to be registered[1] : " that is, the Court of Rome still claims the power of deciding whether the laws of the land are to be obeyed or not, and modern Romanists, whatever may have been the sentiments of their ancestors a century ago, obey the Pope rather than the State.

[1] For my knowledge of these events I am indebted to Purcell's *Life of Cardinal Manning*, vol. ii. pp. 115, 116. An interesting letter of Manning to Mons. Talbot which states the cardinal's views on this subject is given at p. 127.

THE PROTESTATION.

We, whose names are hereunto subscribed, Catholics (1) of England, do freely, voluntarily, and of our own accord, make the following solemn declaration and protestation.

Whereas sentiments unfavourable to us, as citizens and subjects, have been entertained by English Protestants, on account of the principles which are asserted to be maintained by us and other Catholics, and which principles are dangerous to society, and totally repugnant to political and civil liberty; it is a duty that we, the English Catholics, owe to our country as well as to ourselves, to protest, in a formal and solemn manner, against doctrines that we condemn and that constitute no part whatever of our principles, religion, or belief.

We are the more anxious to free ourselves from such imputations, because divers Protestants, who profess themselves to be real friends to liberty of conscience, have, nevertheless, avowed themselves hostile to us, on account of certain opinions which we are supposed to hold. And we do not blame those Protestants for their hostility if it proceeds [as we hope it does], not from an intolerant spirit in matters of religion, but from their being misinformed as to matters of fact.

If it were true that we, the English Catholics, had adopted the maxims that are erroneously imputed to us, we acknowledge that we should merit the reproach of being dangerous enemies to the State ; but we detest these unchristian-like and execrable maxims : and we severally claim, in common with men of all other religions, as a matter of natural justice, that we, the English Catholics, ought not to suffer for or on account of any wicked or erroneous doctrines that may be held by any other Catholics (2), which doctrines we publicly disclaim, any more than British Protestants ought to be rendered responsible for any dangerous doctrines that may be held by any other Protestants, which doctrine they, the British Protestants, disavow.

First, we have been accused of holding, as a principle of our religion, that princes excommunicated by the Pope and council, or by authority of the see of Rome, may be deposed or murdered by their subjects or other persons (3).

But, so far is the above-mentioned unchristian-like and abominable position from being a principle that we hold, that we reject, abhor, and detest it, and every part of it, as execrable and impious; and we do solemnly declare, that neither the Pope, either with or without a general council, nor any prelate, nor any priest, nor any assembly of prelates or priests, nor any ecclesiastical power whatever, can absolve (4) the subjects of this realm, or any of them, from their allegiance to his majesty King George the third, who is, by authority of Parliament, the lawful king of this realm, and of all the dominions thereunto belonging.

Secondly, we have also been accused of holding, as a principle of our religion, that implicit obedience is due from us to the orders and decrees of Popes and general councils; and that therefore if the Pope, or any general council, should, for the good of the Church, command us to take up arms against government, or by any means to subvert the laws and liberties of this country, or to exterminate persons of a different persuasion from us, we [it is asserted by our accusers] hold ourselves bound to obey such orders or decrees, on pain of eternal fire.

Whereas we positively deny (5) that we hold any such obedience to the Pope, and general council, or to either of them; and we believe that no act that is in itself immoral or dishonest can ever be justified by or under colour that it is done either for the good of the Church or in obedience to any ecclesiastical power whatever (6). We acknowledge no infallibility (7) in the Pope; and we neither apprehend nor believe that our disobedience to any such orders or decrees [should any such be given or made] could subject us to any punishment whatever. And we hold and insist that the Catholic Church has no power that can, directly or indirectly, prejudice the rights of Protestants, inasmuch as it is strictly confined to the refusing to them a participation in her sacraments and other privileges of her communion, which no Church [as we conceive] can be expected to give to those out of her pale, and which no person out of her pale will, we suppose, ever require (8).

And we do solemnly declare that no Church, nor any prelate, nor any priest, nor any assembly of prelates or priests, nor any ecclesiastical power whatever, hath, have, or ought to have, any jurisdiction or authority whatsoever within this realm that can, directly or indirectly, affect or interfere with the independence, sovereignty, laws, constitution, or government thereof; or the rights, liberties, persons, or properties of the people of the said realm, or of any of them, save only and except by the authority of parliament;

and that any such assumption of power would be a usurpation (9).

Thirdly, we have likewise been accused of holding, as a principle of our religion, that the Pope, by virtue of his spiritual power, can dispense with the obligation of any compact or oath taken or entered into by a Catholic; that therefore no oath of allegiance, or other oath can bind us; and consequently that we can give no security for our allegiance to government.

There can be no doubt but that this conclusion would be just if the original proposition on which it is founded were true; but we positively deny that we do hold any such principle.

We do solemnly declare that neither the Pope, nor any prelate, nor any priest, nor any assembly of prelates or priests, nor any ecclesiastical power whatever, can absolve us, or any of us, from or dispense with the obligation of any compact or oath whatsoever (10).

Fourthly, we have also been accused of holding, as a principle of our religion, that, not only the Pope, but even a Catholic priest has power to pardon the sins of Catholics at his will and pleasure; and therefore that no Catholic can possibly give any security for his allegiance to any government, inasmuch as the Pope or a priest can pardon perjury, rebellion, and high treason.

We acknowledge also the justness of this con-clusion, if the proposition upon which it is founded were not totally false. But, we do solemnly declare, that, on the contrary, we believe that no sin whatever can be forgiven at the will of any Pope, or of any priest, or of any person whomsoever ; but that a sincere sorrow for past sin, a firm resolution to avoid future guilt, and every possible atonement to God and the injured neighbour, are the previous and in-dispensable requisites to establish a well-founded expectation of forgiveness (11).

Fifthly, and we have also been accused of hold-ing as a principle of our religion, that no faith is to be kept with heretics (12); so that no govern-ment which is not catholic can have any security from us for our allegiance and peaceable behaviour.

This doctrine, that faith is not to be kept with heretics, we reject, reprobate, and abhor, as being contrary to religion, morality, and common honesty ; and we do hold and solemnly declare, that no breach of faith with any person whom-soever, can ever be justified by reason of, or under pretence, that such person is an heretic or an infidel.

And we further solemnly declare, that we do make this declaration and protestation, and every part thereof, in the plain and ordinary

sense of the words of the same, without any
evasion, equivocation, or mental reservation
whatsoever (13).

And we appeal to the justice and candour of
our fellow-citizens, whether we, the English
Catholics who thus solemnly disclaim, and from
our hearts abhor, the above-mentioned abominable and unchristianlike principles, ought to be
put upon a level with any other men who may
hold and profess those principles.

NOTES.

1. It need hardly be pointed out that the title of Catholics commonly claimed by the English Romanists is a misnomer. The Catholic Church in this country is that body which traces its origin up to Augustine, and which has lived an unbroken life from that day to this. The Romanists, as has been shown in the Introduction, are a modern schismatic body, dating from 1570.

2. The fallacy of this argument is not perhaps evident at once. Protestants, including in the term, as the authors of the Protestation did, all who have rejected the claims of the papacy, are divided into many separate bodies, holding no intercommunion with one another, and in no way bound by one another's teaching. On the other hand, Romanists throughout the world form one elaborately organized whole, with the same code of laws, the same discipline,

D

the same authoritative dogmatic teaching, and all looking up to the same head on earth. While it would, therefore, be absurd to assume that a Scotch Presbyterian holds the same doctrine as a member of the Church of England, it is perfectly reasonable to argue from the teaching that prevails amongst Romanists on the Continent to the beliefs of Romanists in England.

3. Cf. the Introduction, pp. 16, 17.

4. On this point cf. the Introduction, p. 18.

5. There can be no doubt that this statement is directly opposed to authorized Roman teaching. The extent of the obedience due to papal and other decrees, according to that teaching, may be seen from the following extracts from the *Moral Theology* of S. Alfonso di Liguori :—

" The Canon Law is included in five volumes, of which the first is the *Decretum* of Gratian, &c., &c. These volumes are established by the holy statutes of popes and councils, and undoubtedly have the force of law."

" It is asked here, first, whether the Decrees or Epistles, Answers or Declarations of the pontiff, which are not inserted in the Corpus [i. e. the above-mentioned collection of Canon Law] have the force of binding law ? The answer is given in the affirmative from the chapter Si Romanorum 1 Dist. 19, where Pope Nicholas V expressly declares it."

" It is asked in the second place whether the
Declarations of the Sacred Congregation of
Cardinals have the force of law? There is no
doubt but that they bind in law in those particular cases for which they are made. . . . The
doubt is whether they bind in similar cases.
There are two opinions, both probable, as the
Salamanca doctors rightly say, n. 28 *in fin.* The
first opinion asserts that such declarations, if
they are fortified by the seal and subscription of
the most eminent cardinal prefect, have the
force of binding law, because the cardinals have
the power of making declarations from the
Pontiff, as follows from the Bull 74 Sixti V. It
is no obstacle to this that they have not been
promulgated, because it is new law that requires
promulgation and not declarations concerning
laws already promulgated."

" It is asked in the third place whether Civil
Laws bind in conscience? On this point, which
it is very necessary to understand, we must here
notice some of the chief considerations. Some
civil laws are expressly approved by the Canon
Law, some expressly corrected, some indeed neither
approved nor rejected. Hence we must say :
(1) Laws that are approved without doubt bind
in conscience. . . . (2) Civil Laws which are corrected by the Canon Law do not at all bind in
conscience. . . . (3) Civil Laws which are not

condemned are tacitly approved by Canon Law [1]."

What this seems to come to is simply this, that any Englishman who accepts the authority and teaching of the Roman Church acknowledges an authority that binds in conscience, and which is able to abrogate any of the laws of the land that may be obnoxious to it.

6. The principle here laid down, that the end does not justify the means, or, in other words, that it is not lawful to do evil that good may come, is taught very emphatically by St. Paul in Romans iii. 8 and elsewhere. It is indeed the clear teaching of Christ and the whole New Testament, and is a fundamental principle of sound morals, but it is not the accepted teaching of Roman moralists. "It is to be remembered that the Jesuits are the most active controversial body in that [i. e. the Roman] Church, and also its chief teachers of morals, either through the work of their own colleague, F. Gury, or through those of Liguori and Scavini, who, though not Jesuits themselves, did but adopt the Jesuit method and principles. But the maxim that 'the end justifies the means' is formally asserted by more than one leading Jesuit theologian and casuist. Thus Busenbaum states it twice in the following terms:—'When

---

[1] Lib. i, Tract ii, *De Legibus*, cap. i. 104, 106.

the end is lawful, the means also are lawful.'
' He to whom the end is lawful, to him the
means also are lawful.' Layman, another
eminent Jesuit, puts it thus in his *Moral
Theology* :—' To whom the end is permitted,
the means adapted to that end are permitted
also '; and Wagemann, a third Jesuit, states it
more sweepingly: 'The end determines the
rectitude of the act [1].' "

7. Cf. the Introduction, p. 28 ff.

8. It is interesting to compare this with the
teaching of accredited Roman theologians. In
De Fide, Disputatio XXIII, Suarez treats fully
of the punishments that may be inflicted on
heretics. He writes as follows :—" But it is
necessary to notice that these corporal punishments are various ; they can, however, be reduced
to four heads. Of this sort are punishments of
imprisonment, not indeed of that imprisonment
which precedes sentence by way of custody, for
that is not punishment, but a necessary means
of examining the cause and discovering the
truth ; after sentence, indeed, it is inflicted by
way of punishment, either for a time or for ever—
that is, for life. And in the same way we do not
count torture amongst these punishments, because
it is inflicted not for punishment but for the

---

[1] Littledale's *Plain Reasons against joining the Church of Rome*,
pp. 207, 208.

discovery of the truth. The second punishment is exile : for it is counted amongst corporal punishments, especially when it is exile to the galleys that is inflicted. The third is flogging or some similar corporal suffering. The fourth is the punishment of death, which, in law, is usually said to be the last punishment ; and we must be specially careful about this, because, if it can be inflicted justly, *a fortiori* so can the rest." Then, after noticing various errors, he goes on : " Nevertheless the Catholic assertion is, that the Church can justly punish heretics with the penalty of death. . . . And this is proved shortly, because two things only are necessary in order that any punishment may be justly inflicted : first, that the punishment should be proportioned to the magnitude of the offence, and, secondly, that it should be inflicted by one who has power and jurisdiction : and both these are found in this punishment." Again : " I say that this power [i. e. of inflicting death on heretics] belongs in a certain way to both courts [i. e. the civil and the ecclesiastical]. It resides truly in the ecclesiastical magistrate, and especially in the Pontiff, and that in an eminent degree. In kings and emperors and their ministers it is as it were proximate, and in subordination to the spiritual power. The former statement is established by the custom of the Church, because this punishment is contained in civil laws and is approved in the canons, as I shall show in a following section [1]."

The doings of the Inquisition in the sixteenth and seventeenth centuries are the logical carrying out of the accepted Roman teaching as set forth by Suarez and others. They are so well known that there is no need to dwell on them, but it seems worth while to notice that the Holy Office was still at work in Spain at the time when the Protestation was drawn up. It is true that its operations were on a very reduced scale. Torture had been given up, and the executions reduced to two or three a year; but still they went on, and did not cease till 1826, in which year a Jewess and a Quaker schoolmaster were put to death. If the Church of Rome has become tolerant, it is because the changed circumstances of Europe have deprived her of the power of persecution. In the Syllabus of 1864 Pius IX condemned the opinions that " the Church has not the right of employing force: she has no temporal power, direct or indirect," and that " in the present day it is no longer beneficial for the Catholic Church to be considered as the only religion of the State, to the exclusion of all other forms of worship, whence it has been wisely provided by the laws, in some

[1] *Works*, vol. xii. pp. 577 f.

countries called Catholic, that strangers going
to reside there shall enjoy the public exercise of
their own forms of worship."

9. Cf. the Introduction, p. 38 f.

10. This statement is no doubt a fundamental
principle in all sound morals. The inviolability
of promises and oaths is at the basis of all sound
civil society, but it is not the principle commonly
adopted by Roman moralists. Their teaching
may be illustrated by a passage from the *Moral
Theology* of S. Alfonso di Liguori.

"In how many ways," he writes, "can the
obligation of a vow be removed? In two ways:
(1) Without the intervention of any one's
authority, and that either by the change of
matter [as if the matter had been before good and
became bad or indifferent, or an obstacle to a
greater good, owing to a new circumstance, or
prohibition, or absolutely or morally impossible],
or by the cessation of the condition on which it
depended. (2) By the intervention of human
authority, and that in three ways, by irritation,
commutation, and dispensation. This is the
common opinion. Hence you may conclude,
that, although it is by your own fault that the
matter has become impossible, unless, &c., yet,
since it has become so, the obligation ceases and
it is enough to be sorry for your fault." iv. 225.

"Dispensation is the absolute doing away

with the obligation of a vow, and is made in the name of God. Good reason is required for its validity, such as : (1) The good of the Church, or the common welfare of the republic, and even of a family, or the greater advantage of the man who has vowed. (2) A notable difficulty in observing the vow. (3) Imperfection of act, or levity, or easiness from which the vow proceeded." iv. 250.

"Those who can dispense are the following : (1) The Pope, with respect to all the faithful. (2) A Bishop, with respect to those under him, but not a parish priest. (3) Regular Prelates, who are exempt, in respect to their monks and novices. . . . By privilege from the Pope, the confessors of the Mendicant Orders, subject to the permission and regulation of their superior." iv. 256 [1].

11. There is no need to give quotations to prove that this statement expresses what is and always has been the teaching of the Church on the subject of Absolution, but at the same time there is little doubt that the belief condemned in the Protestation has prevailed largely in the Roman Communion, and has been to a very great extent the practical guide of life. Two causes

[1] Further information may be found in the *Moral and Devotional Theology of the Church of Rome*, by the Rev. F. Meyrick, M.A. (London, 1857). It is from this work that I have taken the quotations in this and the following note.

seem to have done much to produce this result.

i. The system of Indulgences. There are two penalties attaching to sin—the temporal punishment in this world inflicted by the Church by way of penance, and the vengeance of God in the world to come. The latter, it has been always taught, can only be escaped by true penitence ; that is, by unfeigned sorrow for sin followed by confession, the resolution of amendment and requital made to the best of our power to those whom we have injured: the former, however, is different. It is laid on by the Church for the purpose of helping amendment of life, and therefore if the Church sees fit it can be taken off again. Hence arises the system of indulgences. These are grants of relief from the penance ordinarily attached to sins, and are obtained by payments of money for Church purposes, by performing acts of devotion, by going on pilgrimage, &c. The theory may look plausible, but in practice the distinction between the temporal and eternal punishment of sin is easily forgotten, and when indulgences are to be had freely—as they are in the Roman communion—a lowering of the sense of moral obligation soon follows, conscience is deadened, and men come to commit acts of wrong without thinking.

ii. The doctrine of Probabilism in morals

does much to produce the same result. There are many occasions constantly turning up in actual life when it is not easy to decide the question of right and wrong. The discussion of these cases has given rise to the science of casuistry, and, as might be expected, there are many questions on which different casuists have given different opinions. Which are we to follow? In answer to this question the Jesuits developed the doctrine of Probabilism; that is, that any opinion in morals that has been held by one or more grave doctors, is in itself probable, and that any one may act upon it with a safe conscience, and if in confession a penitent can show that he has acted on a "probable opinion" even though the confessor may utterly reprobate it he can compel him to give him Absolution. One or two passages from the *Moral Theology* of S. Alfonso di Liguori will show to what this doctrine may lead, because after the most careful examination the highest authority at Rome has declared that there is nothing in his writings worthy of condemnation or contrary to sound morals, that on the strength of that judgement he has been canonised as a Doctor of the Church and therefore, whatever decision he has given on any question of morals is certainly a "probable opinion."

The following has reference to evidence given

in a court of justice. " Bonacina says that if a
witness has sworn to speak the truth, he is bound
to speak it on the grounds of justice, because
an obligation of justice arises from an oath and
a promise : but with greater probability Lessius
contradicts him, because a witness swearing that
he will speak the truth, does not intend to bind
himself to declare it on grounds of justice, but
only by virtue of religious scruple." *Moral
Theology*, v. 270.

Again :—" Is the husband bound to keep or
support his wife if her dowry has not been paid ?
The Doctors in common say No, if it is the
fault of the promiser that it has not been paid.
So Sanchez, Bonacina, Bossius, the Salamanca
Doctors, Fagundez, Trulenchius and others, saying
that the object of the dowry is that the husband
may keep his wife with it. Except however (1)
if the husband married without a dowry being
promised, and (2) if the wife pays obedience to
her husband, for then he is at least bound to
keep her like a servant. So say the Salamanca
Doctors, with Abbas, Lupo, &c., quoted by
Sanchez. Sanchez, however (with Surdus and
others) does not allow the second exception,
because [as he says] the wife is bound to pay her
husband both a dowry and obedience, and therefore it is not necessary for him to maintain her
if she only pays obedience. But I rather adhere

to the opposite opinion, because the law of nature itself teaches you to keep one who occupies himself in being your servant." L. vi. 939.

"But if a man has the intention of gradually enriching himself by a number of little thefts, committed on one or many, or of doing great harm, he sins gravely in that intention; and though each act is only venial in itself, yet, as it subserves to such an intention, it is, on the whole, the commission of a mortal sin, because men do grave damage to the community, and that practice is very pernicious to human society, e. g. if a tailor purloin a little piece of cloth from different persons, or if tradesmen use too short measures, &c. . . . Meantime they [i. e. the tailors, tradesmen, &c.] are sometimes excused from grave sin. (1) From what has been said above. (2) If they act as they do for the sake of indemnifying themselves, or because they would otherwise make no profits, or because they ought to raise their price, and then would not find customers. (3) If otherwise, they have not means of supporting themselves and those belonging to them." L. iv. 533.

"But what if a nobleman is very much ashamed to beg or to work, can he provide for himself out of other people's goods? The Salamanca doctors say No, with Soto and Prado, on the ground that this must be rather counted grave than extreme necessity, temporal goods being ordained only for preserving life, not for keeping honour. But Viva says Yes, and Roncalglia and Mazzotta, as well as Lessius, Palao, and Diocastillo in Croix: so do Bennez and Serra. And this seems to me the ' more probable,' if he is so ashamed of begging that he would rather die than beg." L. iv. 520.

12. Cf. the Introduction, p. 25.

13. This statement is emphatic enough, and would seem to exclude all possibility of prevarication or wish to deceive on the part of those who signed the Protestation ; and, so far as the narrative in Butler's *Memoirs* goes, there is nothing to suggest that this was not the case. It appears, however, that there was some difficulty in securing the names of the Vicars-Apostolic. " We have it on the authority of Mr. Butler, that all the Vicars-Apostolic at first made some difficulty about signing the Protestation [1]. They did indeed afterwards sign it, but Bishop Walmsley complained that he was surprised into his signature and withdrew it. Bishop Matthew Gibson directed that if ' his name was absolutely necessary, it should be affixed by Bishop James Talbot, *in sensu Catholico* [2].' "

[1] Husenbeth's *Life of Milner*, p. 23, quoting from Butler's " Red Book," fol. 14.

[2] *The History of Catholic Emancipation*, by W. J. Amherst, S.J., vol. i. p. 164.

What did Bishop Gibson mean by signing *in sensu Catholico*? Are we to understand it as implying that he signed not in " the plain and ordinary sense of the words " of the Protestation, but only so far as the statements in the Protestation were in accordance with the accepted teaching of the Church? If so, it would seem that when he signed he meant to give his sanction to the direct contrary of most of the propositions which he seemed to approve. The quotation given above, in Note 10, from S. Alfonso will show, however, that since the cause—the good of the Church—which induced him to sign was a valid one, he could be dispensed from any obligation that his signing might lay upon him.

THE END.